How do I say that?

Written by **Sue Wise**
Illustrated by **Christine Coirault**

Editor: Annabel Blackledge
Editorial Director: Louise Pritchard
Design Director: Jill Plank

Pangolin Books and Sue Wise would like to thank Lena Münch, German
assistant at Pate's Grammar School, Cheltenham, for her help with the text.

First published in the UK in 2005 by Pangolin Books
Unit 17, Piccadilly Mill, Lower Street, Stroud, Gloucestershire, GL5 2HT

A CIP catalogue record for this book is available from the British Library.

ISBN 1-84493-023-8

Colour reproduction by Black Cat Graphics Ltd, Bristol, UK
Printed in China by Compass Press Ltd

Contents

The German language

There are a few things you should know about the German language before you try to speak it. Take a few minutes to read the information below, and you will enjoy this book all the more.

Masculine, feminine, neuter, plural

All German nouns are masculine, feminine or neuter. If a word has *der* (**the**) or *ein* (**a**) in front of it, it is masculine. If a word has *die* (**the**) or *eine* (**a**) in front of it, it is feminine. And if a word has *das* (**the**) or *ein* (**a**) in front of it, it is neuter. The endings of these words may change slightly according to which part of the sentence they are in. Plural nouns, whether masculine, feminine or neuter, have *die* (**the**) in front of them. The spelling of some plural nouns differs from the singular spelling.

There are lots of capital letters in German because all nouns begin with a capital letter.

das Haar
hair
Haar is neuter.

die Zähne
teeth
die is used for plural nouns.

die Hand
hand
Hand is feminine.

der Fuß
foot
Fuß is masculine.

How verbs change

German verbs change according to the subject of the sentence (the person who is doing the action). Some verbs follow regular patterns, but others do not. You will find that the verbs *sein* and *haben* are used often in German. These lists will help you recognize them.

spielen – to play
(a regular verb)
ich spiele (**I play**)
du spielst (**you play**)
er/sie/es spielt (**he/she/it plays**)
wir spielen (**we play**)
ihr spielt (**you play**)
Sie spielen (**you play**)
sie spielen (**they play**)

sein – to be
(an irregular verb)
ich bin (**I am**)
du bist (**you are**)
er/sie/es ist (**he/she/it is**)
wir sind (**we are**)
ihr seid (**you are**)
Sie sind (**you are**)
sie sind (**they are**)

haben – to have
(an irregular verb)
ich habe (**I have**)
du hast (**you have**)
er/sie/es hat (**he/she/it has**)
wir haben (**we have**)
ihr habt (**you have**)
Sie haben (**you have**)
sie haben (**they play**)

Saying it in German

- Read the pronunciation guides beneath the German as if they were English.

- The pronunciation guides divide some words with hyphens to make it easier to say them.
- All the letters in German words are pronounced clearly.
- Two dots above a vowel is the German *Umlaut*. It changes the way the vowel sounds.
- In the pronunciation guides, say the letters 'yur', as in 'tyur' – *Tür* (door), like 'ure' in the English word pure.
  - When you see a 'u̲' in the guides, as in 'hu̲nt' – *Hund* (dog), say it like the 'oo' in the English word foot.
- In German, the letter 'w' is pronounced 'v', as in *Wasser* (water), which is pronounced 'vasser'.
- The letter 'z' sounds like 'ts', as in *Zehen* (toes), pronounced 'tsayen'.

- The German letter 'ß' sounds like the 'ss' in the English word hiss.
- When a 'g' comes after an 'i' in German, it makes a 'sh' sound, as in *sanftig* (juicy), which is pronounced 'zanftish'.
- The German 'r' sound is said in the back of the throat.
- In many German words, 'ch' sounds like the 'ch' in the Scottish word loch, as in *Buch* (book). This sound is written as 'ch' in the pronunciation guides – 'booch'.
- In some German words, 'ch' sounds like the 'sh' in the English word shell, as in *Milch* (milk). It is written as 'sh' in the guides – 'milsh'.

Fangen wir an.
Fangen veer an.
Let's get started.

Norbert's thoughts

Norbert the dog always has something amusing on his mind. When you see a thought bubble in German, try to guess what Norbert is saying to himself.

Then turn to page 32 to find out if you are right. Different countries have different sayings, so you may be surprised when you discover exactly what Norbert is thinking!

Lotti, Markus und Norbert essen das Frühstück.

Lottee, Markus <u>u</u>nt Norbert essen dass frooshtook.

der Schrank
dayer shrank
cupboard

der Kühlschrank
dayer kewlshrank
fridge

die Butter
dee b<u>u</u>tter
butter

die Eier
dee eyer
eggs

die Schale
dee sharler
bowl

die Krawatte
dee kravatter
tie

die Leine
dee liner
dog lead

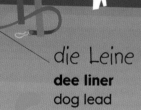

Wo ist mein Frühstück? Ich habe einen Bärenhunger!

die Milch
dee milsh
milk

die Cornflakes
dee cornflakes
cereal

die Marmelade
dee marmelarder
jam

Vati
Fartee
Dad

die Tasse
dee tasser
cup

Mutti
Muttee
Mum

der Herd
dayer hairt
cooker

der Löffel
dayer lerfel
spoon

der Kaffee
dayer kafay
coffee

das Messer
dass messer
knife

der Stuhl
dayer shtool
chair

die Aktentasche
dee aktentasher
briefcase

der Orangensaft
dayer oronjhenzaft
orange juice

7

Kannst du mein **Messer** putzen? Es ist auf den Boden gefallen.

Kanst doo mine messer putsen? Es ist owf dayn bohden gefallen.
Can you clean my knife? I dropped it on the floor.

Schalte den **Herd** ab! Das Essen brennt an!

Shallter dayn hairt ap! Dass essen brennt an!
Turn off the cooker! The food is burning!

Das Brot schmeckt viel besser mit **Butter**.

Dass broat shmeckt feel besser mit butter.
Bread tastes much better with some butter.

Vati isst sehr gern Erdbeer**marmelade**.

Fartee ist sayer gairn airdbayer-marmelarder.
Dad adores strawberry jam.

Ich habe meine Schulbücher auf dem **Stuhl** vergessen. Setz dich nicht auf sie!

Ish harber miner shool-bewsher owf daym shtool fer-gessen.
Zets dish nisht owf zee.
I left my school books on the chair. Don't sit on them!

Mutti sagt die **Milch** ist sehr gut für die Knochen.

Muttee zargt dee milsh ist zayer goote fyur dee knochen.
Mum says that milk is brilliant for your bones.

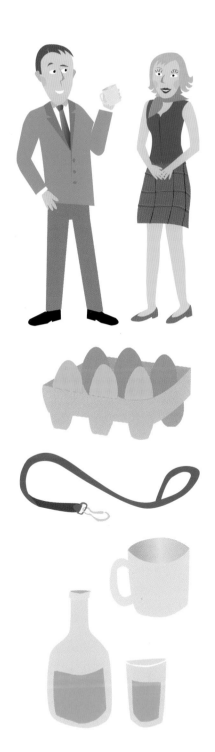

Mutti macht jeden Morgen mein Frühstück – sie ist sehr nett.

Muttee macht yayden morgen mine frooshtook – zee ist zayer net.

Mum makes my breakfast every morning – she is very kind.

Vati kommt immer zu spät zur Arbeit.

Fartee kommt immer tsoo shpait tsewer arbyte.

Dad is always late for work.

Ich esse gern gekochte **Eier** zum Frühstück.

Ish esser gairn gekochter eye-er tsum frooshtook.

I like boiled eggs for breakfast.

Wo ist die Hunde**leine**? Es ist Zeit für seinen Spaziergang.

Voh ist dee hunderliner? Es ist tsight fyur zynen shpat-seer-gang.

Where's the dog's lead? It's time for his walk.

Mutti trinkt zwei **Tassen** Tee vor der Arbeit.

Muttee trinkt tsv-eye tassen tay for dayer arbyte.

Mum drinks two cups of tea before work.

Jeden Morgen trinke ich ein Glas **Orangensaft**.

Yayden morgen trinker ish ine glass oronjhenzaft.

Every morning, I drink a glass of orange juice.

Alle Kinder sind in der Klasse und sind fleißig.

Aller kinnder zint in dayer klasser <u>unt</u> zint flyssish.

der Goldstern
dayer goltshtairn
gold star

die Zahlen
dee tsahlen
numbers

das Lineal
dass linayarl
ruler

der Globus
dayer glob<u>u</u>s
globe

die Kugelschreiber
dee koogelshryber
pens

der Computer
dayer komputer
computer

die Maus
dee mouse
mouse

die Tastatur
dee tastatooer
keyboard

die Lehrerin
dee lairerin
teacher

das Fenster
dass fenster
window

die Tür
dee tyur
door

die Uhr
dee ooer
clock

die Garderobe
dee garderober
cloakroom

die Zeichnung
dee tsighshnung
drawing

die Bleistifte
dee blyshtifter
pencils

der Fisch
dayer fish
fish

der Tisch
dayer tish
table

das Aquarium
dass akwahrium
fish tank

das Flugzeug
dass floogtsoyk
aeroplane

Ich bin eine wirkliche Leseratte!

11

Die Lehrerin wird *böse* mit uns, wenn wir aus dem **Fenster** sehen.

Dee lairerin virt burzer mit unts, venn veer ows daym fenster zayen.

The teacher gets cross with us if we look out of the window.

Ich kann gerade Linien ohne ein **Lineal** nicht zeichnen.

Ish kan gerarder leenyen ohner ine linayarl nisht tsyshnen.

I can't draw straight lines without a ruler.

Wo sind die **Kugelschreiber**? Ich muss meine Handschrift üben.

Voh zint dee koogelshryber? Ish muss miner hantshrift ewben.

Where are the pens? I need to practise my writing.

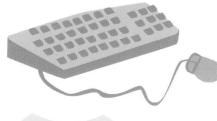

Ich kann auf der **Tastatur** tippen, ohne auf sie zu gucken.

Ish kan owf dayer tastatooer tippen, ohner owf zee tsoo gucken.

I can type on the keyboard without looking.

Der **Fisch** wohnt in einem Aquarium.

Dayer fish vohnt in eye-nem akwahrium.

The fish lives in a fish tank.

kannst du mir deinen roten **Bleistift** leihen?

Kannst doo mere dinen rohten blyshtift lion?

Can you lend me your red pencil?

Ich habe eine tolle **Zeichnung** eines Fisches gemacht.

Ish harber eye-ner toller tsyshnung eye-ness fishess gemacht.

I have done a brilliant drawing of a fish.

Schau mal auf die **Uhr** – es ist fast Mittagessen!

Show mal owf dee ooer – es ist fasst mittag-essen!

Look at the clock – it's nearly lunchtime!

Schau dir mal Deutschland auf dem **Globus** an!

Show deer mal doitshlant owf daym globus an!

Look at Germany on the globe.

Kannst du die **Tür** zumachen? Es ist kalt.

Kannst doo dee tyur tsoomachen? Es ist kalt.

Can you close the door? It's cold!

Die **Lehrerin** sagt mir mein Heft ist nicht sehr sauber.

Dee lairerin sargt mere mine heft ist nisht zayer zowber.

The teacher tells me that my notebook is not very neat.

Jeder möchte einen **Goldstern** bekommen.

Yayder mershter eye-nen goltshtairn bekommen.

Everyone likes getting a gold star.

Lotti und Markus gehen zum Supermarkt mit Mutti.

Lottee unt Markus gayen tsum zupermarkt mit Muttee.

die Kekse
dee kekser
biscuits

die Tomate
dee tomarter
tomato

der Kuchen
dayer koochen
cake

der Lutscher
dayer lutcher
lollipop

die Bohnen
dee boanen
(tinned) beans

der Käse
dayer kayzer
cheese

die Banane
dee bananer
banana

die Karotte
dee karrotter
carrot

Ich habe nicht genug Geld für einen Kaufrausch!

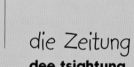

die Zeitschrift
dee tsight-shrift
magazine

die Zeitung
dee tsightung
newspaper

das Spülmittel
dass shpewlmittel
washing-up liquid

das Angebot
dass angerboat
special offer

das Hundefutter
dass hunderfutter
(tinned) dog food

das Fahrrad
dass far-rat
bicycle

die Kasse
dee kasser
(checkout) till

der Schinken
dayer shinken
ham

das Geld
dass gelt
money

der Einkaufswagen
dayer ine-kowfsvargen
trolley

15

Lutscher sind nicht gut für die Zähne!

Lutcher zint nisht goote fyur dee tsayner!

Lollipops are not good for the teeth!

Kannst du mir diese Zeitschrift kaufen?

Kannst doo mere deezer tsight-shrift kowfen?

Will you buy this magazine for me?

Der Einkaufswagen hat ein quietschendes Rad – es hört sich aus wie eine Maus!

Dayer ine-kowfsvargen hat ine queetchendes rat – es hurt sish ows vee eye-ner mouse!

The trolley has a squeaky wheel – it sounds like a mouse!

Es gibt Angebote überall im Supermarkt.

Es gibt angerboater ewberal im zupermarkt.

There are special-offer signs all over the supermarket.

Lass nicht den Hund den Schinken stehlen!

Lass nisht dayn hunt dayn shinken shtaylen!

Don't let the dog steal the ham!

Vergiss nicht das Hundefutter – der Hund hat Hunger!

Fer-gess nisht dass hunderfutter – dayer hunt hat hunger!

Don't forget the dog food – the dog is hungry.

Ich habe mein **Fahrrad** draußen gelassen. Hoffentlich wird es nicht regnen!

Ish harber mine far-rat drowssen gelassen. Hoffentlish virt es nisht raygnen!

I've left my bicycle outside. I hope it doesn't rain!

Mutti sagt wir dürfen keine **Kekse** kaufen.

Muttee sargt veer dewrfen kyner kekser kowfen.

Mum says we can't buy any biscuits.

Mutti hat am Freitag **Kuchen** zur Arbeit mitgenommen.

Muttee hat am Fry-tag koochen tsur arbyte mit-genommen.

Mum took some cakes to work on Friday.

Ich habe mein ganzes **Geld** für Bonbons ausgegeben.

Ish harber mine gantsers gelt fyur bonbons ows-gegayben.

I have spent all my money on sweets.

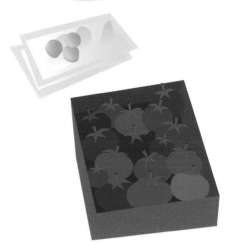

Wir brauchen keine **Tomaten**.

Veer browchen kiner tomarten.

We don't need any tomatoes.

Sollen wir **Käse** für Butterbrote kaufen?

Zollen veer kayzer fyur butterbroater kowfen?

Shall we buy some cheese to make sandwiches?

Sie gehen mit Norbert zum Park für ein Picknick.

Zee gayen mit Norbert tsum park fyur ine pick-nick.

die Schaukel
dee showkel
swing

die Rutsche
dee rutsher
slide

die Wippe
dee vipper
seesaw

der Teich
dayer tiech
pond

der Fahrradhelm
dayer far-rat-helm
bicycle helmet

die Limonade
dee limonarder
lemonade

die Äpfel
dee epfel
apples

die Chips
dee ships
crisps

das Skateboard
dass skateboard
skateboard

der Schlamm
dayer shlamm
mud

das Brot
dass broat
bread

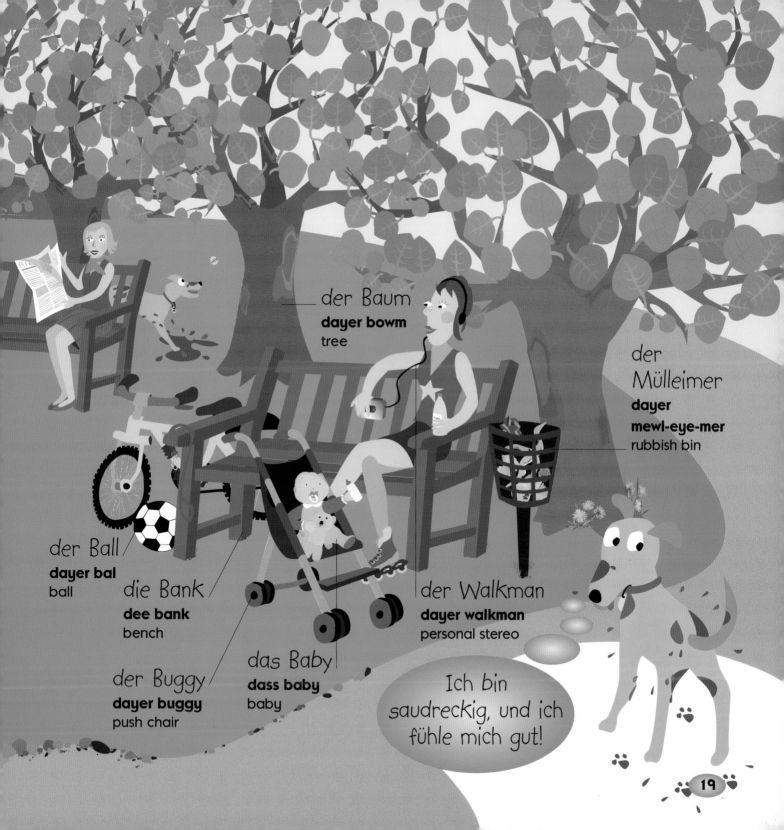

der Baum
dayer bowm
tree

der Mülleimer
dayer mewl-eye-mer
rubbish bin

der Ball
dayer bal
ball

die Bank
dee bank
bench

der Walkman
dayer walkman
personal stereo

der Buggy
dayer buggy
push chair

das Baby
dass baby
baby

Ich bin saudreckig, und ich fühle mich gut!

19

Die **Bäume** sind toll zum Versteckspielen.
Dee boymer zint toll tsum furshteck-shpeelen.
The trees are great for playing hide-and-seek.

Willst du mich an der **Schaukel** anschubsen?
Villst doo mish an dayer showkel anshubsen?
Will you push me on the swing?

Ich habe Hunger. Darf ich etwas **Brot** essen?
Ish harber hunger. Darf ish etvass broat essen?
I'm hungry. Can I have some bread?

Wo ist Mutti? Sie ruht sich auf der **Bank** aus.
Voh ist Muttee? Zee root zish owf dayer bank owss.
Where's Mum? She's having a rest on the bench.

Mmm, diese **Äpfel** schmecken sehr gut, ganz knackig, süß und saftig.
Mmm, deezer epfel shmecken zayer goote, gants knackish, zews unt zaftish.
Mmm, these apples are delicious, all crunchy, sweet and juicy.

Ich spiele gern mit dem **Ball**, besonders wenn ich ein Tor schieße.
Ish shpeeler gairn mit daym bal, bezonders venn ish ine tor sheesser.
I like playing with the ball, especially when I score a goal.

Was trinken wir beim Picknick?
Die **Limonade**, natürlich.

Vass trinken veer byme pick-nick? Dee limonarder natyurlish.
What are we drinking at the picnic? Lemonade, of course.

Es tut weh, wenn ich von meinem
Skateboard falle.

Ess toot vay, venn ish fon my-nem skateboard fal-ler.
It hurts when I fall off my skateboard.

Nimm den Abfall und bring ihn in den **Mülleimer**!

Nimm dayn ab-fal unt bring een in dayn mewl-eye-mer!
Pick up that rubbish and put it in the bin!

Mein Hund spielt gern im **Schlamm** –
das macht ihm viel Spaß!

Mine hunt shpeelt gairn im shlam – dass macht eem feel shpass!
My dog likes playing in the mud – he thinks it's fun!

Iss den Eis nicht auf der **Wippe**!

Iss dayn ice nisht owf dayer vipper!
Don't eat ice cream on the seesaw!

Beim spielen **Chips** essen – das ist verrückt!

Bime shpeelen ships essen – dass ist feroockt!
Eating crisps while playing – that's crazy!

Später baden die Kinder den Hund.

Shpairter barden dee kinnder dayn h<u>u</u>nt.

Ich hätte lieber eine Katzenwäsche – ich hasse Baden!

der Wasserhahn
dayer vasserharn
tap

die Zahnbürste
dee tsarnbewrster
toothbrush

die Hose
dee hozer
trousers

das Boot
dass boat
boat

das Waschbecken
dass vashbecken
basin

die Unterhose
dee <u>u</u>nterhozer
pants

der Kamm
dayer kam
comb

das Halsband
dass halsbant
collar

die Dusche
dee doosher
shower

der Schaum
dayer showm
bubbles

das Radio
dass rardeo
radio

das Handtuch
dass hand-tooch
towel

die Toilette
dee toyletter
toilet

das Shampoo
dass shampoo
shampoo

der Schwamm
dayer shvamm
sponge

die Badewanne
dee bardervanner
bath

die Badematte
dee bardermatter
bathmat

die Seife
dee zyfer
soap

die Ente
dee enter
duck

die Wasserpistole
dee vasser-pistoaler
water pistol

23

Mutti hat mir gesagt, ich soll mir die Hände im **Waschbecken** waschen.

Muttee hat mere gesargt, ish zoll mere dee hender im vashbecken vashen.

Mum told me to wash my hands in the basin.

Die Flasche **Shampoo** ist fast leer.

Dee flasher shampoo ist fasst layer.

The bottle of shampoo is nearly empty.

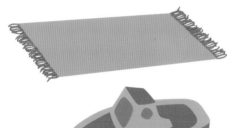

Die **Badematte** ist ganz nass! Wer hat gespritzt?

Dee bardermatter ist gants nass! Vayer hat geshpritst?

The bathmat is all wet! Who's been splashing?

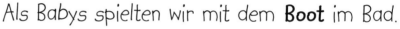

Als Babys spielten wir mit dem **Boot** im Bad.

Alss babies shpeelten veer mit daym boat im bat.

We used to play with the boat in the bath as babies.

Der Hund mag es, wenn wir sein **Halsband** abnehmen.

Dayer hunt mak es, venn veer zine halsbant ap-naymen.

The dog likes it when we take off his collar.

Hör zu! Dein Lieblingslied ist im **Radio**.

Her tsoo! Dine leeblings-leet ist im rardeo.

Listen! Your favourite song is on the radio.

Lass nicht den Hund mit der **Ente** spielen!

Lass nisht dayn hunt mit dayer enter shpeelen!

Don't let the dog play with the duck!

Ich habe meine **Zahnbürste** verloren.

Ish harber miner tsarn-bewrster fer-loren.

I've lost my toothbrush.

Es ist gut, sich mit einem weichen **Handtuch** zu trocknen.

Es ist goote, sish mit eye-nem vyshen hand-tooch tsoo trocknen.

It's good to dry yourself with a soft towel.

Ich spiele gern mit meiner **Wasserpistole**.

Ish shpeeler gairn mit miner vasser-pistoaler.

I love playing with my water pistol.

Ich mag ein Bad mit viel **Schaum**.

Ish mak ine bat mit veel showm.

I like baths with lots of bubbles.

Vati sagt, wir müssen uns beeilen. Er will die **Toilette** benutzen!

Fartee sargt, veer mewssen unss be-eye-len. Ayer vill dee toyletter benutsen!

Dad says we have to hurry up. He wants to use the toilet!

Es ist Zeit ins Bett zu gehen.
Jeder ist hundemüde.

Ess ist tsight inz bett tsoo gayen.
Yayder ist hunder-mewder.

die
Rakete
dee
rakayter
rocket

das
Poster
dass poster
poster

die Baseballmütze
dee baseballmewtser
baseball cap

die Comics
dee comics
comics

die Leselampe
dee layzerlamper
lamp

Wenn ich nicht
schlafe, bin ich ein
Morgenmuffel.

die Socke
dee zocker
sock

der Turnschuh
dayer toornshoo
trainer

der Wecker
dayer vecker
alarm clock

die Puppe
dee pupper
doll

die Perlen
dee pairlen
beads

das Tagebuch
dass targerbooch
diary

das Buch
dass booch
book

der Teddybär
dayer teddybear
teddy bear

das Glas Wasser
dass glass vasser
glass of water

das Bett
dass bett
bed

das Nachthemd
dass nacht-hemt
nightshirt

die Bürste
dee bewrster
hairbrush

der Pantoffel
dayer pantoffel
slipper

das Federbett
dass fayderbett
duvet

Ich möchte **Poster** in meinem Zimmer aufhängen.
Ish mershter poster in my-nem tsimmer owf-hengen.
I like putting up posters in my bedroom.

Mein Lieblings**buch** ist sehr Komisch!
Mine leeblinks-booch ist zayer kohmish!
My favourite book is very funny!

Es ist nützlich ein **Glas** Wasser neben dem Bett zu haben.
Es ist newts-lish ine glass vasser nayben daym bett tsoo harben.
It's useful to have a glass of water by the bed.

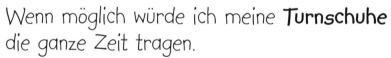

Wenn möglich würde ich meine **Turnschuhe** die ganze Zeit tragen.
Venn merglish vurder ish miner toorn-shooer dee gantser tsight trargen.
I'd wear my trainers all the time if I could.

Mein **Teddybär** ist weich und Knuddelig.
Mine teddybear ist vysh unt knudderlish.
My teddy bear is soft and cuddly.

Man kann Geheimnisse in ein **Tagebuch** schreiben.
Man kann ge-hyme-nisser in ine targerbooch shryben.
You can write secrets in a diary.

Diese **Socken** riechen wirklich schrecklich!

Deezer zocken reechen virklish shrecklish!

These socks smell really bad!

Meine Katze mag auf meinem **Bett** schlafen.

Miner katzer mak owf my-nem bett shlarfen.

My cat likes sleeping on my bed.

Ich muss meinen **Wecker** stellen – morgen ist Schule.

Ish muss my-nen vecker shtellen – morgen ist shooler.

I must set my alarm clock – it's school tomorrow.

Wir lesen oft **Comics** bis spät in die Nacht.

Veer layzen oft comics biss shpayt in dee nacht.

We often read comics late at night.

Hast du meine **Bürste** gesehen? Meine Haare sind sehr verknotet.

Hast doo miner bewrster gezayen? Miner hahrer zint zayer ferknohtet.

Have you seen my hairbrush? My hair is really tangled.

Meine **Pantoffeln** halten meine Zehen mollig warm.

Miner pantoffeln hal-ten miner tsayen mollish varm.

My slippers keep my toes cosy.

Index

Is there a particular word you'd like to learn in German? This index features all the key words found in the book (in English followed by the German translation) as well as lots of other useful and interesting words selected from the sentences and Norbert's thoughts.

Norbert's thoughts!

p.6 Wo ist mein Frühstück? Ich habe einen Bärenhunger!
Vo ist mine frooshtook? Ish harber eye-nen bearen-hunger!
Where's my breakfast? I've got a bear-hunger! (I'm starving.)

p.11 Ich bin eine wirkliche Leseratte!
Ish bin iner virklisher layzer-ratter!
I'm a real reading-rat (bookworm).

p.14 Ich habe nicht genug Geld für einen Kaufrausch!
Ish harber nisht genoog gelt fyur eye-nen kowfrowsh!
I haven't got enough money for a buying rush (shopping spree)!

p.19 Ich bin saudreckig, und ich fühle mich gut!
Ish bin zow-dreckish, unt ish fewler mish goote!
I'm sow-dirty (filthy), and I feel good!

p.22 Ich hätte lieber eine Katzenwäsche – ich hasse Baden!
Ish hetter leeber eye-ner katsenvesher – ish hasser barden!
I'd rather have a cat-wash (quick wash) – I hate having a bath!

p.26 Wenn ich nicht schlafe, bin ich ein Morgenmuffel.
Venn ish nisht shlarfer, bin ish ine morgen-muffel.
If I don't sleep, I will be a morning-sourpuss. (I will be grumpy in the morning.)